1st edition

ISBN 0-917488-03-2

LC 77-089528

Available from Ziesing Brothers
768 Main Street, Willimantic, Conn. 06226

JAMES SCULLY

SCRAP BOOK

ZIESING BROTHERS
WILLIMANTIC CT
1977

Some of these poems have appeared in, or under the auspices of: *Hudson River Anthology, Jack the Ripper, Liberation News Service, The Minnesota Review, Occum Ridge Review, Praxis, Quechua Peoples Poetry* and *The Radical Teacher.*

Particular thanks are due to Alexander Taylor and the Curbstone Press, and to Maria A. Proser for help in translating 'Testament: Fragments' and the two poems by Alejandro Romualdo.

'With Awful Luck' is by an Aztec survivor of the Spanish Conquest.
The Quechua song lyrics (transcribed and translated into Spanish by Jesús Lara) are from the Cochabamba region of Bolivia. They are more or less contemporary. 'In Cuzco' and 'American Love' were written in Peru, October 1973.

'Elementary School' was written in Santiago de Chile, under the dictator-ship imposed by Chilean reactionary forces in complicity with the United States and Brazilian governments.

for john,
juanito

'Come Up With Me, American Love'

Neruda

The slaves drive the iron and the steel
Through the streets, through the iron fields.

I ride a condor who devours
North America, my children, my flowers.

Dope kills and so to bed.
Dope kills the world instead.

Regal, naked, I rise and wander
High as carnival the empty slums, my condor

Hovers
        I mount the Western imagination like bronko Amigo

And fly fly fly away

Grandin Conover
1937-1969

WINTER JOURNAL

I'd sat alone in the Sistine Chapel
as in an old barn

So bone creeping cold
even the guards had gone.

Against the Judgment wall Michelangelo crumpled
his own skin like a trophy

Adam, waking, had already dreamed the God
rather than face himself . . .

What went wrong? that we'd got up to make
a masterpiece of our misery.

The sky, if it had feeling, would also grow old
wrote Chairman Mao.

The guards, they guarded a stove in the storage room
thawing their fingers and toes.

THE TREASON OF THE CLERKS

Our blood rose
          as sap through a system,
Like the civil service of Chinese men of letters
working their way up.

A few of course refused
          to live by the rules.
Grandin skipped class, holed-up writing
          As The Hawk Sees It
His only set, the U.S. Embassy
          shook like a future refugee: Berlin 1936
as the hawks seized it.
When the manuscript was stolen
          with a suitcase full of clothes
He went ragged, wrote another year.
That finished his career.
All he found written in his book
          was treason
               Graffiti like
'Art and Science are your only seasons
Pray use them as switchblades, like a poet,
          not as wallets or semesters.'

And Tu Fu failed the Imperial examinations
twice.
The establishment . . . his best
          poetic prose couldn't get him in.
Grandin couldn't pass
          an I.Q. test for the draft
He fell asleep instead.
And took off for parts unknown
               again again

Nine years later, the chief medical examiner
            City of New York
forwarded his opened letter.
The message?
            'The unquestioned
is the only answer there is.'

            Nevertheless
Neil and I among others
            passed with flying colors
We were
            a heartwarming disgrace
like conscripted soldiers who have won a war.
When he inscribed *The Dream That Was No More A Dream*
            (about the Third Reich
                        as theatre come to life)
Neil called it his coloring book.
Graduated into a think tank
He tried to breathe
            ethics into computers
humanism into universities.
Which took like a vaccine.
They were immune.
                        Daemonic
he designed and rehearsed a scenario
            —Totalitarian Classroom—
                        so true to life
it was like getting an education.

What I did
            was higher learning.
Was paid to do it, to people
            who could pay to have it done.
Public education
            it didn't cost much,
Just enough to keep the dirt
poor out.

Those who were well-off, wore privilege
like fatted calves
They had everything
        anyone would think to have.
The best of them
                tossed and turned
Like Adam, dreaming he would share
        the awful windfall of Eden

                Only
the years pass.
The day came
        I sat among the students, refused to speak
5 minutes, 10—
Across the room
a girl I thought I knew
                screamed
'What do you want us to do!'

It's cold mornings,
        I get up
it's another age.
                I'm at court, a tutor
spanking the princes who could make him eat grass
—no not princes
        pillows stuffed with insurance.
Beautiful
        boys and girls
they smile, spoiled.
Why should they be so complacent, so bruised
        sitting there.
I talk down
                pouring out words: for ruined children
the future of the middle class.

Jayne above all . . .
Rainy days
        her hair
sprang ringlets to show Dante the light
                the mere glimmer of it
Held in a classroom where the windows had gotten dark,
        whole semesters gone up in cigarette smoke,
She wanted this
        lecture parading as discussion
conducted outside.
Spring
        spring before
She'd had a Sociology class
                    out in the apple orchard
'Petals were falling
        all over us
on our heads and shoulders
between the pages of our books . . .'

I would go anywhere with her.

I didn't turn a hair.

Already the night air smacks of fall
Each weekend the flurry of parties
        piles up, thicker and more brilliant.
Strange. When Tu Fu got the censor's job, even then
        his children starved.
How many?
Chronicles won't say.
Our lives as leaves grow
             glorious sickening on the sugar maples,
First light touch of spring
        pails cling to them
greedy, draining the sweet.

And his last job, adviser to a petty warlord in Szechuan
well after the An Lu-shan rebellion
      he drifted away from.
Under the cold stars, the same
      Tu Fu who once shared a blanket with Li Po
as though they were brothers.
He went down the Yangtze.
He might be a log
      except for the poetry,
With different versions of his death
passed down
      by word of mouth.
And of his family, nothing more is heard . . .

This mouth would move
      once, only when it wished.
Three winters
      in the summer cottages, we shivered
by a kerosene stove.
We were green students.
4 a.m. one night
      Neil walked across the frozen lake
just to talk.

Now he jets
      clear over the Atlantic
Only they pay him
      to keep talking.
They pay me well.
Having had
      misfortune to pass the exams
Tu Fu had the misfortune
to fail.

And yet, so
             what.
We are the evergreens, too!
Cool odd points
             our stunned warbling calls 'a climax forest'
Under sunlight, the headlong gusts of rain
             loaded with snow dripping down . . .
We're affected,
not changed.

Today a Russian woman asked
             'Where's your intelligentsia?'
I say, mine is yours
All times
             everywhere.
It serves every passing master
             or it doesn't. That may not matter.
   What does is
we give cold comfort to one another,
like whippoorwills sounding the night.

Neil, old distant friend
             more bird of feather than friend—
And Tu Fu whose brush strokes
             bleeding out each bud, leaf, cumulus
                          rose to meet the elements—
And that other friend
             mounting the western imagination, inviting me
O to fly away—

the beauty is,
between this earth and that sky
we owed nothing to no one,
        All along
                        green as needles, shoulder by shoulder
with everything that lives,
we were paying our way with lives

WE ARE THE EVERGREENS, TOO

for Mel

And if, under a sky gone gray at the temples,
       snowflakes as pencil shavings
mount a glittering heap,
And each day pulls a longer shadow
           as the drawer of a filing cabinet—

If with that our limbs cracked, oozing sap
       and we cry out
Still, nothing new happens

Or someone comes with gloves on
to brush the snow off your shoulder

You get goose-bumps, your hairs bristle
       because you are touched
You sing
       you whisper, no
you sing
moved

And if in the moody sea-green sweep of the wind
or is it a shudder
       blond green sprouts
stiffer than flowers,
it's spring

Out of my mouth
       the breath flies, a tiny gray flurry
which may as well be a tufted titmouse
       showing the spot of rust by its breast,
or the dull orange sun bleeding through a cloud
whose burning crest may be our witness

16

NORTH END

Hartford, Connecticut
16 years old, two children
                    struggling alone

Peaches, I tell it cold as I can.
That winter's morning you stared out the window
                    into the filthy
                                        wind
            the honey colored slum
you said, as though saying nothing

'when I wake up in the morning
I don't want to wake up'

HALFWAY INTO PARADISE

1
Halfway into Paradise
        Dante hears
the advice he wants to hear:
'Tell the whole truth.
No lies.
If it stabs them
        sick, even to tears
let them pick at their own scabs.'

That's what I say

I say that.

2
Now I hear
        a pure spirit or wise guy
put this burning question to Chou En-lai:
Why. Why didn't he
        push the revolution to the hilt
and finish the job.
Chou replied, 'Look here
        look at my mother.
She has bound feet.
What can she do
        but hobble around.
If I cut them loose, she would fall down.'

That's what I say

I say that.

3

So torn the gut

howls in the pit

INNOCENCE

Like any brute, to have a soft heart.

To be the last benevolent despot
or revolutionary without arms.

Imprisoned by Bonaparte
to embrace Sade,

to spit out, as he did,
'At least *I* never killed anyone'

To have thought that good
or good enough.

Like any beast, to have dreamed
murder begins or ends

in flesh and blood.

So. To have sought like a dog
panting with peace and love

Or bought a man or woman
however thrilled or willing the ruin

To have used a piece of human.

To didn't mean to do it
and be sincere.

You held yourself pure
regardless.

You thought you were the motto?
You were the money.

And once upheld the Universal Declaration of Human Rights,
forgetting to feed the cat.

A man and woman of principle
a real shit

to have been wishful,
for ever and ever

To have sung your starry ideal
lulling as an alibi

Evening news rocked like a bedtime story

so awful and graceful
it had no moral.

You had been above all
impartial

Every question, like genocide,
had at least two sides

every question a burning answer.

You wept at the blood,
washed and wept

for the good it did.

Bitter at the end,
guilt was your pride and joy

because you were shameless.
You had no sense of shame.

You were no solution.
You were you.

My heart went out to you
as an executioner,

it did what it had to do.

You could not, could not tell
my heart from my hand.

SEIZE THE DAY

Women I had
            like swatting houseflies.
Men know what that meant
Knocking off a piece

Screwing it to death
                        I came
            I saw stars.
There wasn't a soul around.

Nights were pure murder
            like slumming, 5 banged her out in the car
One bitch I robbed.
Drunk as lords
            we dropped bills all over the black-&-tan bars,
Money the ultimate muscle.
We figured that much.
Brain matter mixed with leaves, that color
                        Dollars
anyone can smell the perfume of
            drugged them to their knees,
Subtler than the swish of aerial whips . . .
The way Aztec warriors used to mill about
            singing flower wars
To kill with flowers

I danced my ass off
            into the small hours.
High, in concert we
            stomped a guy to the floor.
Terror.
            And taking off, peeling rubber, fired
Twice, missed!

Shadows rushing out
                    froze.
It was a nightmare,
no one got hurt.

It was night all day.
Balls chafed
            young and sore
a gang dragging through the city,
Whoever got away?
Cock erect
            like an insomniac,
no future in that.
We lived though
            like there was no tomorrow

I never knew sorrow.

I sang with the cats
Here pussy here
                    pussy pussy pussy fur
the way a jet screamed over sopping jungle
                    throttling it
To no end.
There was none
            only surroundings.
Dusk glared all night
            down the violet lighted avenues, even
Greenery swallowed
            all we drove into it.
Spunk, rubbers, junked cars aflame
forgotten as last month's clap, drip, hot . . .
            we were
amnesic as pain.

My god like a scar
          feeling nothing
I was ecstatic.
I gave it all I had

OVER IRISH COFFEE

In the cliff house, above the Pacific
where it breaks up
        We watched
through the saltglazed window,
Masses of water
        slopped at the seastacks, the winded
breakers grew finer and whiter

And talked, giddy and sober
over Irish coffee
        At Enrico's I poured
icewater on his head,
When I got home
        he was a drunken stupor
sprawled all over the bed,
He'd melted our wedding rings
        into a gold lump
and buried it in the garden
to no end
but this blooming confusion

Something was giving though:
smalltalk
        about to go over the hill,
back and forth
        it staggered
like bees in April, about
to recall what flowers are

the feast was all around us.

I had this with her, a muse
          who has little use for art.
She'd been around. She knew
how fragile passion grows.
And simpler,
wilder too

Gigolos
          you have a high time with,
but it's the boy nextdoor who breaks your heart

POOR. PARADISE.

Coming at last
into our own land,
we were
where we are

Alone together in another slum,
bristling
            like cactus glory in the desert,
We too
            erect were bliss
We wished only for what is.
My heart was in your mouth
Blood under your skin was juice
            easing my lips
Our word came forth naked
courting what is.
What is
            blessed us, blessing enough for us.

One human being was no human being.

In our tribe everyone starved
or no one did

PARADISE

There are no men, no women,
there is human

Without irony,
because what's left to wish for

Making love is more
than poor stick buried in a hole.

Finger-tips dance over buttocks and breast
as ants through the fresh-turned earth

So thoroughly into life
we need not describe it anymore

TRANSLATIONS 1973
plus 2

WITH AWFUL LUCK

With awful luck, pained we saw our pain.

Broken lances
lie in the roads,
hairs are scattered about.
The houses are roofless,
their walls hot
red hot.
Worms sprout through the streets and plazas,
the walls are flecked with brains.
Waters are red, red as if dyed,
and if we drank
it was saltpetred water.
TERRIFIED WE BEAT AT THE MUD WALLS
and we were left with our heritage:
a net of holes.
We put our lives behind our shields,
but shields do not hold off
the desolation.
We have eaten crumbs of bird seed,
we have chewed bitter dog grass,
adobe chips, small lizards, mice
and ground up earth and even worms . . .

(Aztec, c. 1521/28)

NOTHING?

Alone like this I have to go?
Like the flowers that perish?
And nothing left of my name?
My fame here on earth? Nothing?

At least the flowers! at least the songs!

(from: Cantos de Huexotzingo)

SONG OF THE SPIRIT

                              Spirit, little grandfather,
little old man with the face of a mouse,
the tip of the nose moth-eaten,
the backbone a long saddlesore,
the mouth spouting drivel,
the palm begging to be greased,
the left eye always running,
the right ear broken off,
little foxy with its tail tangled up,
vicious little runt of an ass—

that's you as you are, Spirit,
little old man with the face of a mouse

                              (contemporary Quechua folksong)

WHAT ARE THESE

                              What are these?
They're senators! that for
a mingey salary
will start a war

                              Mariano Baptista
the great speechmaker
I stick on the rooftops:
that tightfisted milker

                              Mendizabalcito
has plunged into the mud
ah! but he's gotten up
all covered with gold

                              Look at that
senator, look inside him:
nothing! No, but
his pockets are stuffed

                              The priest of Mizque
has written me, saying:
Senators!? You might as well
cut off their balls

                              Mendizabalcito
has fallen into the water, ah
but he's gotten out again
dry as a bone

Senators of the valley
can't find their tongue,
because they don't have one
they cultivate their fingernails

Every mother's son
lives on his land, in his house.
Only I, poor exile
have no home no homeland

What Jiménez de Asúa said
is clearer than pure water:
Among our presidents, is where
the biggest thief will be

(contemporary Quechua folksong)

36

WHAT CLOUD IS THAT CLOUD

What cloud is that cloud
gathered so close?
Probably my mother's tears
turning to rain

I'm a man traveling alone,
I have no mother no father,
until even the tree by the road
is a tree that gives no shade.

Bringing me into the world
my mother said: 'You will be a man.'
And father: 'You'll be a worker
and a slave,' he said. And wept.

Between this day and the next
I leave on a long journey.
If there's life, I can come back.
If death, not ever again.

Purely by chance, I have a mother
that I may have a father
that he may say, some day:
'Where is my son?'

(from a contemporary Quechua folksong)

TESTAMENT: FRAGMENTS

                   Let end in me, the three
hardships of the world:
to be lonely, to be poor,
to live in someone else's house.

                   To have to go uphill
zigzag, by the z of the road,
and at each z
stop, and burst into tears.

                   Here you have it: my orange
grown in a graveyard.
You see what my misery is,
what I endure in the world.

(from a contemporary Quechua folksong)

BEAUTY PARLOR

Gold
and misery
of Peru. Parlor
of horrors
and beauty. I have said,
seen
and heard, with my soul
clinging to the earth. I see—
being born in blood, the face
of the rose, in night the day, in afternoon a sky
wide open as the carcass of a steer, the gold
pure under the sky of gold.
I see
the sun
being born, the day
dying, daily, in flames,
and this is the same—or almost the same—
as a graveyard of living rot.
And the sea
goes on, the sea rolling round
like a hoop in the sea, the sky
face down, I go on seeing
and hearing
drenched children in the streets, begging
bread
they pay only thank-you for, good-bye for
the misery received.
Everything
muttered, all
disjointed, lying there, broken,
I see
misery coated with smiles, meals
eaten off newspaper, and I hear

the sun from a silent bell
sounding out
against me, against everyone,
for having pointed the poem into the ulcer
the parlor
(of beauty and horror) in which we endure.

(Alejandro Romualdo, Peru)

FIST & LETTER

Put
the letter
in your fist: Write, write, write
against wind and tide, against shadow,
against this whole horrible masquerade
that passes daily before our eyes.

Put
your fist
in the letter: And blot, blot, blot out
the blood buckling us in, the shadow
spilled across the soul, the terrifying
misery
that peoples the face of charity.
Strike
with the letter.

Put
your mouth
at the bottom
of this pit: And sing, sing, sing
truths you can put in your fist.

(Alejandro Romualdo, Peru)

41

IN CUZCO

Something they had to celebrate,
                              so came
                 bundled in ponchos
the sodden color of old copper,
and in alpaca skullcaps
              with pom poms
with earflaps curling up ¡ay!
and bare feet, cardboard shoes, in suit jackets
   round-shouldered as the cobblestones,
and highdomed panama hats
              painted white,
white with a black band,
                      and in petticoats,
in chemical blue
tennis shoes

a trumpet they had, flutes
beating at skin
              drums and a bass drum too,
and placards waved in the dusk: as though
              swatting at bats
                      with wands,
brushing away the Cerro Corporation,
              its yanquis, its paper
   deeds
rattling their chains in the dark . . .

Dispossessed of all
but original insolence
                (the heart in its ribs
          like a bloody rag in a fist)
they quick-stepped
                    through the cold wet street,
hupping and fluttering a red flag

Peru, X.73

AMERICAN LOVE

We did not sacrifice
the human, but had

40 and more
kinds of potatoes,

a few to spread out
on strewn wet grass

these we left: 4, 5 nights
to freeze on the top ridge

and each morning, underfoot
squeezed the moisture out

till they were hard as rocks
and kept for years,

but soaked in warm
water an hour or more

they softened and swole
they made a stew

and no one starved,
we always had food

we never had to say
I love you

Peru, X.73

44

WASHINGTON TO SANTIAGO 1973
SANTIAGO TO WASHINGTON 1976

ELEMENTARY SCHOOL

Santiago de Chile, X.73

Why is it the trivial saying
warbles with rage, and tears.

Shaken. *This is the rain*
that kills the little birds.

She said birds, she meant
children.

And the rain was weapons
inspecting the books,

the rain was dollars, a hush
scudding across the earth

the rain was workers, peasants, it was misery
raining fear, blood, dirt.

What after all was rain
but the lesson—

that birds were children
the wind blew, the rain struck and slurred . . .

until the children learned
they were not children,

nor rain rain,
birds birds

POSTSCRIPT

Washington, Sept. 21 — Orlando Letelier, who was foreign minister in the Chilean government of President Salvador Allende Gossens, was killed here today when a bomb exploded in his car as it sped along fashionable Embassy Row.

A woman assistant to Mr. Letelier was killed and a third person injured.

Mr. Letelier was a leader of Chilean political exiles in this country who oppose the military junta that overthrew President Allende in 1973.

—The New York Times

One last word for Orlando.
But what? word will do
justice
to the man nicknamed 'Fanta,'
the diplomatic
gentleman with moustache, the receding
tabby colored hair—
where's the *bajativo*
for humor
that outmaneuvered pathos!
Where is it
that passed across the table
as banter, or better yet
butter
between Orlando
and García Márquez?
Where is that word now.
And the other,
that legal word
mincing other legal words
to kiss off the piranhas—
where is that one!

Frazzled in Paris?
with Neruda
pumping spitballs and jokes
down the solemn conference table?
With Pablo then? whispering
those hands shuffling paper
murder people

Or was it the
word sprung from prison
calling long distance:
who ever dreamed
a man in a concentration camp
but in a poem, too!
would step out one day, bother
getting in touch to say
                    thank you,
        I was moved by your poem
He was moved? We were humbled.
Words were real after all!

Yet where is the soft firm
hugging word
for Isabel, his wife,
and their 4 strong boys?
Where
for José, Chris, Pancho,
for Pablo always
away with grandmama . . .
Where was it
September 21st, 1976,
when that
old
frost blue Chevy

the split second it sounded
like water on a hot wire

as that same
car like any other
rolled down Embassy Row
by Sheridan Circle: when
his legs were gone
and his beautiful life.

His wasn't the only life.
When he died, when his beloved Allende died,
assistants and workers
by thousands with hard hands
or soft hands,
all
naked hands,
lay mangled by their side.
Where then was the word
word
reform, where the peaceful
road to socialism,
the sad
bourgeois comedy of blood!

The word DINA didn't exist,
no yellow pages listed
CIA, not one word rose waving over
the payroll of Cuban
worms winding through their corridors—
coming out, that morning, to murder Orlando
before squirming back.
No word for that.

But for Orlando
whose blood ran from offices and ledgers
into the street,
word came at last.
For Orlando, who once did dance
in Caracas

and in Georgetown.
For Orlando
who'd gone too far, whose gut
breath burst the chains
of his own
wretched expensive class.

He did not say this.
He did not have to say it.

Around his death his
life was joining in, by 2's and 3's, by more, and much,
so much life
raising dragging banners, placards, passing out leaflets
even in Hartford, Connecticut, U.S.A.
And the word began to chant
                    COMPAÑERO ORLANDO LETELIER
and the word sang back
                    ¡PRESENTE!
is HERE . . . is
no more
gone to negotiate
life with piranhas and worms—

but here
on the street
of arms linked in arms,
with Hectór, Juan, Bessy, with
Elsa and little Franco
milling and marching, like it or not, his life now sings
through us
who salute with our fist:
that no comrade may be lost,
that together we are all
present! Orlando, present, and in this
struggling love accounted for.

TO THE SONG OF RESISTANCE
ONLY REVOLUTION DOES JUSTICE

AL CANTO DE LA RESISTENCIA
SOLO REVOLUCION HACE JUSTICIA